Heal Your Home, Fix Your Life! The easy guide to Love and Money

Heal Your Home, Fix Your Life! The easy guide to Love and Money
© Copyright by Angela Wilde
2010.
First edition
All rights reserved.
ISBN 9781453707555

All rights reserved under International Copyright Law.
No part of this book may be stored or reproduced in any form without the express written permission of the copyright holder.

www.angelandpsychicbooks.com

Contents

1. Introduction   5

2. A - Z   7

3. You're on your way to health, wealth and love!   89

1. Introduction

This book is for those people who want results fast, and with little effort! It's said that if your life has gone bottoms up due to Feng Shui being off the mark in your home, fixing a few little things will get amazingly fast results.

If my books stop selling well, I look around the house, and lo and behold! One of the kids will have left empty soda bottles in the middle of the spare room, or suchlike! Every time! And every time I clean out and smudge the house, the books sell like crazy! But I'm getting ahead of myself here.

Lots of people can't afford to have a complete Feng Shui consultation, or even know the year their home was built. They just want something that works, and fast. This book, however, is not just about Feng Shui – it's about every easy (and safe!) spiritual thing to do to your home that will have a profound impact on your life.

Energy is important. When the energy in your home is flowing happily, your life too will flow happily. Little blocks in your home reflect as blocks (sometimes not so little!) in your life. The five elements appear as yin (shadow, feminine) or yang (light, masculine), transform into the six energies, and take form as natural aspects of the land. Water and earth are yin, and mountains and sky are yang. When your whole environment is in harmony, there is good energy (called Sheng Chi), but when the energy is out of balance it is negative energy (called Sha Chi), and this is energy to be avoided. Good chi, energy, also means taking care of your environment, and taking care of nature.

The idea is to live in harmony with our environment so that the energy works for us and not against us.

The good thing is, if the energy in your home is what is preventing love and/or money coming to you, then fixing the energy will have very fast results!

To make it easier for you I have put it in alphabetical order.

2. A - Z

ABUNDANCE

Abundance is about all good things, not just about money, but either way, to have abundance whether financial or not, your house needs to be free of dirt, mess, dust, and clutter!! I myself am not someone who would normally enjoy cleaning for the sake of it, but I have seen for myself the direct result of a spotless house on finances, and now I am a cleaning fanatic! I tell you, it works!

The South East part of your house is the Wealth sector, so make sure this is gleaming, dust free and spotless, and no clutter there, even in drawers.

AFFIRMATIONS

Affirmations MUST be stated in the PRESENT TIME, not at some future date – you need to speak out that you have it NOW. If you affirm, "I want a new car," that means it will be in the future, and will stay there, in the future! You need to say, "I have new car *now*."

Don't worry if you find affirmations hard to say at first. Some people even have strong reactions and may even get upset or cry when they first say affirmations. That's fine, it's just the process of changing negative thought patterns. It's important to be consistent when saying affirmations.

As you repeat affirmations over and over they weaken your negative beliefs and enter into your subconscious and become your new beliefs. It doesn't matter if you do not believe what you are saying at first, as this will change. It will also change things in the spiritual realm.

AIR

It is vitally important to get fresh air into your house or apartment. Open all the doors and windows whenever possible. Even in the depths of winter, try to open a window even a little bit as often as you can! This gives the negative energy a chance to escape, and ensures a fresh flow of good chi (energy) into your home.

It is always nice (and beneficial for love and money!) to have lovely scents in your home, and you can use incense sticks or oil burners in which you can burn essential oils. I avoid fragrant oils as to me they smell like chemicals. I love the actual essential oils, and your home will too!

AMETHYSTS

It is ideal to have your bedhead against a solid wall. However, if you cannot manage this and there is a triangular shape behind the bed, it's a great help to place an amethyst geode behind your bedhead. A geode is a big clump!

Amethyst is from the ancient Greek word meaning "not drunken," but I know plenty of people who, shall we say, have a little too much to drink on occasion, and their amethysts don't seem to help much in that regard!

It's also good to place amethysts in your wealth sector, that is, the South East.

AURA CLEANSING BATH

These are fabulous! You will feel a million bucks when you have one of these!

Run a nice bath and into it put a small handful of sea salt and a small handful of Epsom Salts (magnesium sulfate). For full-on aura cleansing, put in a few drops of Sandalwood essential oil. However, you can instead put in Ylang Ylang essential oil or Lavender essential oil. Light a candle and meditate, or even just relax!

ANNUAL ENERGIES

This is to do with "Flying Star" Feng Shui. By the way, they are not actual stars, this is just a term to refer to the energies. The flying stars stay in the house for the year and change at the beginning of each Chinese New Year. There are auspicious stars and inauspicious stars, so you need to know where these are in your home. The two most inauspicious stars are the 5 Yellow Earth Star and the 2 Black Earth Star. For example, in 2009 the 2 star was in the West and the 5 Star was in the North.

I have below drawn up a table of 6 years to give you an idea of how the flying stars change. Other years can be googled. Simply look up and see which sectors of your house are affected by each Flying Star for the year.

The auspicious stars are 1, 4, 6, 8, and 9. The inauspicious stars are 2, 3, 5, and 7. Some say the 9 star can be either auspicious or inauspicious, depending on its circumstances, but I always treat it as auspicious! In the table below, "C" refers to the center (of your house), and the others are compass points, SE for South East (the South East sector of your house), and so on.

Year	1	4	6	8	9	2	3	5	7
2008	C	NE	N	E	SE	NW	W	S	SW
2009	NW	S	SW	SE	C	W	NE	N	E
2010	W	N	E	C	NW	NE	S	SW	SE
2011	NE	SW	SE	NW	W	S	N	E	C
2012	S	E	C	W	NE	N	SW	SE	NW
2013	N	SE	NW	NE	S	SW	E	C	W

All you need to know is where the flying stars are for the year, and what to avoid doing. The 5 star brings bad luck, financial loss, and accidents. The 2 star brings illness, diseases, and serious health issues. To avoid such nasties, do not do any renovation or any ground breaking in the sectors of your home where these stars are in any given year. For Flying Star 2, do not place candles, quartz crystals, metal wind chimes or anything representing earth or fire in that area. For Flying Star 5, avoid fire energy - no candles, and arrange your seating so you do not face this direction. If you are into Feng Shui objects, the 5 Elements Pagoda is a great one for the 5 Yellow Star, as is the 6 rod wind chime. Heavy round metal objects are good to place in both these areas, as are 6 Chinese coins tied with a red ribbon in a row.

Flying Star 3 (Hostile Wood) and Flying Star 7 (Violent Metal) are also inauspicious stars. The 3 star brings fights, law suits, and arguments. The 7 star brings violence, burglary, and severe bad luck. To avoid the 3 star troubles, use lamps, red candles, the colors pink, red, and purple in this area, and avoid metal items, especially metal wind chimes. Do not place a fish tank or other water here. To avoid the 7 star troubles, use the colors blue and black, keep the windows in that sector shut, and avoid candles, quartz crystals, the color red, strong lighting, and metal wind chimes.

Well the good news is that there are favorable stars! The 1 Star (White Water) brings career recognition and promotion. The luck there is activated by the colors blue, black, and gray, and non-sharp metal objects. Avoid candles and the colors red, pink, purple, orange, and lilac.

The 4 Romance Star (Green Wood) is great for writers – it brings literary luck and also love luck. It is activated by plants, flowers, bamboo, paper, linen, silk, cotton, rectangular shapes, a crystal globe, and anything depicting pair of happy lovers, or items which to you symbolize love. Avoid wind chimes, fire colors, and metal.

The 8 Wealth (White Earth) Star brings prosperity and lots of money luck. It is especially good between the years 2004 to 2024. It is activated by quartz crystals especially rose quartz, faceted crystals, any non sharp objects in the amount of eight, the colors red, pink, purple, orange, yellow. Avoid heavy metal objects or wood in this area. If you are into Feng Shui objects, it is good to use a pair of mandarin ducks here.

The 9 Multiplying (Fire) Star multiplies the good luck of the sector and is the star of future wealth. Keep it well lit, and place 9 red or purple candles, the colors red and pink, and don't put out the fire energy with too much water element – such as actual water, or the color blue, wavy patterns or the like.

The Number 6 Heavenly Star (White Heaven) brings success, prosperity luck, and helpful people. A Laughing Buddha is good here. Also use jade, a turtle figure, a jade tree, quartz crystal, and the colors blue, gray and black. Avoid water scenes, red colors, and candles.

ANTIQUES

Objects hold onto energies of past owners. If you love antiques, fine! Just be aware that anything that has been owned by another person will have its own energies.

ART

If you are a single person wanting a relationship, get rid of all artwork depicting single people! No matter what your circumstances, the home should not have sad artwork, even if it's an original Picasso! All images in the home should be uplifting and happy, and should not make you feel unhappy or uneasy in any way. Avoid abstract art that shows distorted images of people or buildings, as this is very bad energy. It is better to have a picture of a sunrise than a sunset. Avoid pictures of dangerous animals, especially in bedrooms.

B

BABY MOBILES

Even if it's a mobile playing Brahms' Lullaby, it is not good to have a moving thing hanging over your baby and can prevent your baby sleeping well. If you must place it over baby, do so at the foot end.

BAGUA

The Bagua mirror is used to deflect negative energy (Sha Chi) such as corners of a building pointing directly at your house, or a tree directly in line with your front door.

Baguas should never be placed inside the home and should be placed over the door (or window) so that it faces out. Never place a Bagua mirror inside a building.

BAMBOO

Chinese lucky bamboo is popular in Feng Shui and is said to bring good luck, financial blessings, youth, and perseverance. Lucky bamboo is grown only in water and just needs its water topped up, and at the least, filtered light to do well. It's a good idea to place lucky bamboo in the South East sector of the home which is the wealth sector. All bamboo is considered auspicious.

BASIL

Basil is a fantastic herb for finances! The Hindu practice of Vastu Shastra holds that basil planted near the house or in a pot inside the house is very favorable. It is generally agreed across cultures that growing basil brings prosperity.

I wash my floors with basil to encourage prosperity – I simmer some in a pot of water, then put that into the floor washing mix! You could instead use basil essential oil.

Basil has been associated over the centuries with attracting wealth, and with protection from negative energies. Some sprinkle it over the entrance to their home to keep out negative influences.

BELLS

Feng Shui uses metal bells for various things such as ringing metal bells in the 5 Star and 2 Star sectors of the house to dispel negative energies. It is also useful to hang 6 metal bells at the front door which will chime when anyone enters or leaves.

BEDS

A second-hand bed is a big no-no! Get rid of your old bed and get a new bed if you have come to the end of a long term relationship, it will do wonders for you!

Whatever you do, don't have two single mattresses pushed together to make up a double bed, European style. This is the very worst thing you can do for a relationship! Also, don't sleep under wooden beams. Water features or paintings which depict water in the bedroom cause financial loss as well as relationship problems. A bottle or glass of drinking water is fine, however.

It is good to put a pillow protector on your pillows. At any rate, it is important at regular intervals to give your pillows a good shake then a thorough wash in a mild, organic washing substance and then put them in the sun to dry and to absorb good chi. The sun is also very cleansing.

I also recommend organic sheets, and I put lavender essential oil in the washing cycle rinse, heavenly! Red sheets bring passion into your love life. If you don't want to have red sheets on display, it will work just as well to have a red sheet over your mattress and under your other sheets!

BED DIRECTION

Now this one is amazing and can bring very fast results! You put the head of your bed on the wall which is in your favorable direction. Now it is not your feet which point to your favorable direction, it is the actual bedhead which must be on the wall of your favorable direction. You have 4 favorable directions, and 4 unfavorable. This is how you find out your favorable directions. You need to find out what is called your "Kua" (also known as "Gua") number.

For Females

Add the numbers of the birth year until it becomes a single number (so 1983 would be 1 + 9 + 8 + 3 = 21). Add until you get a single number. (So in the example of 1983, you would add the 2 + 1 and get 3.)
Add 4 to that single number. (If you end up with a double number, add those numbers together to get a single number.) The Kua number in the above example therefore is 7.

For Males

Add the numbers of your birth year so it becomes a single number (so 1983 would be 1 + 9 + 8 + 3 = 21. Then you would add 2 + 1 and get 3).

Subtract this number from 11. (In the above example, 11-3 is 8.) (If you end up with a double number, add those numbers together to get a single number.)

The Kua number in the example is 8.

Here is a list of your best and worst directions based on your Kua number. It is best if your bedhead is against the wall in your 1st favorable direction which is "Success," or your 4th favorable direction which is "Peace," but any of the 4 favorable directions will do. Avoid at all costs having your bedhead against an unfavorable direction, even if this means that your bedroom door is then behind you. This is preferable in this situation – just keep your door closed!

"Success" is the luckiest direction, and means prosperity, power, and respectability.

"Health" means not only physical health, but also happy relationships and general harmony.

"Romance" means good romantic relationships, as you would expect, but also longevity, optimism, and support.

"Peace" means stability, peace, money saved easily, and family troubles resolved.

"Mishaps" means lack of luck, arguments.

"5 Ghosts" doesn't mean spirits, but stumbling blocks, irritations, relationship problems, accidents, injuries, fire.

"6 Killings" means failed relationships, complaints, malice, jealousy, nasty encounters.

"Total Loss" is very bad, as the name suggests! It means bad luck, disease, loneliness.

Here is a table to calculate your best and worst directions.

Best Directions

Kua	Success	Health	Romance	Peace
1	SE	E	S	N
2	NE	W	NW	SW
3	S	N	SE	E
4	N	S	E	SE
5 Female	SW	NW	W	NE
5 Male	NE	W	NW	SW
6	W	NE	SW	NW
7	NW	SW	NE	W
8	SW	NW	W	NE
9	E	SE	N	S

Worst Directions

Kua	Mishaps	5 Ghosts	6 Killings	Total Loss
1	W	NE	NW	SW
2	E	SE	S	N
3	SW	NW	NE	W
4	NW	SW	W	NE
5 Female	S	N	E	SE
5 Male	E	SE	S	N
6	SE	E	N	S
7	N	S	SE	E
8	S	N	E	SE
9	NE	W	SW	NW

BATHROOM

The cleaner and nicer your bathroom is, the nicer your life will be! Keep it spotless. Keep cosmetic lids dust free. Throw out old cosmetics, they harbor bacteria! Have beautiful soft fluffy towels – if you have kids, you can designate a different colored towel for you and one for the kids. If you have young kids with bathroom toys, store the bathroom toys somewhere! I know, it's hard, but it's so worth it!

Make sure the taps don't leak! Also, keep the door closed at all times, particularly if the door is to a bedroom. Keep the toilet lid down or your money will go down the drain!

Have your bathroom as a sensual place where you can relax. Fill it with fluffy towels, essential oils, and put sea salt and Epsom Salts in pretty jars.

BLACK TURTLE

This is Form School Feng Shui, and refers to the shapes at the back of your house or the back of your apartment building. The Black Turtle is meant to protect the house and give the occupants support. It is favorable to have a mountain, a large building (even another building which is not too much smaller) or a group of trees behind your house or apartment block. Lack of such can mean trouble with superiors at work and/or financial problems – you may find money comes in but does not stay. If you don't have a strong Black Turtle, and you live in a house, build a solid fence or put up some screening, such as bamboo which is cheap and easy to put up. If you live in an apartment, put a painting of a mountain on your back wall.

BEAMS

Exposed beams are usually said to be a problem in Feng Shui as the Chi is supposed to cut into whoever is under them. Try not to have your bed or chair directly under a beam. Some say that bamboo flutes placed in a certain way cut exposed beams, but some Feng Shui masters say not to worry about beams unless you are sitting or lying under one!

BEDROOM

Firstly, no exercise gear in the bedroom, secondly, get that television out of there! Same goes for the computer! It is important to have space either side of your bed, so make sure the side of your bed is not pushed up against a wall – this will adversely affect romance! It is ideal to be able to see the whole room while lying in your bed, and especially the door. It's also good to avoid your feet pointing directly to the door as this is called the "coffin position." However, it is far better to have your bedhead up against the wall which is in your favorable direction, so go for the favorable direction first with these other directions secondary. Closing the door is a Feng Shui cure anyway!

Mirrors must never reflect the bed, as this is said to invite a third party into the relationship. Some Feng Shui masters say to get all mirrors out of the bedroom. However, others say that it is fine if they are there, so long as they do not reflect anything of the bed and provided you are able to sleep well. If you are unable to move mirrors that reflect the bed, cover them. If they are sliding mirrored doors, tape wallpaper to them, or do something to cover them!

Another consideration is to make sure there is nothing stored under the bed, as the occupant is said to absorb the energy of whatever is under the bed. Also, anything under the bed prevents a good flow of chi and this is not good!

If there is a bathroom attached to the bedroom, make sure the door is always closed.

Make sure you have no paintings of single people or unhappy images in your bedroom.

Water in the bedroom can cause relationship loss or troubles as well as money loss. This includes aquariums, paintings of water scenes and so on but it is fine to have glasses of water by the bedside! Just avoid paintings of waterfalls, lakes, and anything to do with water, and especially don't have an aquarium in there!

Everything in the bedroom should be in pairs.

BOOKS

Make sure your books on the bookshelf are very neat and tidy. It's all too easy to pile books in, but this is bad energy. Don't keep books just for the sake of it – give them away to an antiquarian or used bookstore. Too often clutter is disgusted as books! You need to have books on what you want attract into your life, so sad books aren't quite the thing! Books on bookshelves put out negative energy, so don't have them in the bedroom, and it's best to have doors on bookshelves.

BRAS

An old trick is to wear a sprig of lavender (or yarrow) in your bra if you are looking for love! You can add a small piece of rose quartz as well, but experiment until you figure out where to put it, as when I first did this, I had rose quartz falling out all over the place! Rose quartz is good for anyone, whether you are looking for love or if you already have it. Avoid wearing black bras as they darken the heart chakra.

C

CALABASH

The calabash or Wu Lu (also sometimes simply called a gourd) is an ancient Chinese symbol of health, protection, and longevity. The calabash works against sickness energy so is good to place whenever the Yellow Sickness 2 Star is in the particular year. It is also good to place one near your bed to counteract any sickness energy. It is advised to have a natural calabash (which has a hole in the top) rather than a brass calabash or something in the shape of a calabash.

CANDLES

Different colored candles represent different things. Red candles in the bedroom and / or the South West sector of the house represent passion, and pink candles represent romance. Purple candles represent spiritual insight, inspiration, and success, and are good to place in the sector where the 9 Flying Star is for the year. Tall green candles represent wealth, prosperity, and fertility. It is good to place tall green candles in the South East sector of the house for wealth. Yellow candles represent clarity of thought and harmonious communication. Blue candles represent truth, healing, and also communication. Orange candles represent good outcome in legal matters as well as creativity.

Black candles are used to prevent harm, or to get rid of something. White candles represent cleansing and spiritual protection.

Candles are wonderful to have around the house, especially if they are scented!

CAREER

The North sector of your home represents your career sector. If you want your career to flourish, the North must be entirely clutter free and sparkling clean, no dust, no dirt, no cobwebs. Blues and black are auspicious colors. Anything that represents water is good, and wavy lines are good too.

CEILINGS

Low and sloping ceilings are not good in Feng Shui. Try not to sleep under a sloping ceiling. If you have to have your bed there, make sure that your headboard is in the higher area. It also helps to have lighting in the lower part of the ceiling and to leave the light on as much as possible.

CENTER OF THE HOME

This needs to be free of clutter. This is a very important space.

CLUTTER

Clutter in the house will keep success, good luck, happiness, and good relationships from someone! Clutter is the direct enemy of good chi. It's simple, clutter must go! This applies not only to clutter that can be seen, but even clutter in drawers and cupboards.

You can't be too ruthless with clutter. If you haven't worn clothes in a year, donate them to charity or throw them out! Now! If you have books you will never read again, donate them to charity too. Antiques – do they creep you out? Get rid of them! Is there anything from a past sour relationship? Get rid of it! Ok, it might be expensive, so sell it! Just do not keep it. Is there anything that doesn't make you feel good when you look at it? It must go! If in doubt, throw it out!

Before removing clutter, walk around and clap your hands loudly over it. You can bang a spoon on a saucepan instead! Better still ring metal bells or a Chinese singing bowl over it. This no doubt sounds strange, but it actually helps!

COMPASS SCHOOL

In Compass School Feng Shui, you should treat each sector of your house in a certain way.

The North sector of your house relates to career. Moving objects (but not wind chimes) go well here, as do flowers, bamboo, paper, linen, silk, cotton, and green landscape pictures. The colors blue, black, and gray are ideal, as are wavy lines and depictions of water. Avoid metal, and the colors red, white and silver.

The South sector of your house is to do with your fame and reputation, and is the fire element. Colors here are red, pink, purple, but avoid the water energy of blues, and actual water such as aquariums, as this will put out the fire energy. Candles are good here. Keep your cash and jewelry in the South or South West. If it is in a safe, the safe should open towards the North. If you have a wooden framed picture with red as its predominant color, the South is a wonderful place to hang it. This is also a good place for an umbrella, which signifies protection from loss of income.

The East sector is wood element and concerns family relationships and health. Brown and green are good colors here.

Metal is the element of the West sector and good colors are blue, black, gray, and white. Avoid fire colors here, no reds, pinks, oranges, purples. The West sector is all about creativity and children.

The North East sector of the house is the earth element, and relates to the pursuit of knowledge, thus wisdom and learning. Use earth elements here such as ceramic bowls, and a bit of fire energy is good but don't overdo it. Clutter in the North East sector of the house causes loss of wealth.

The South East sector is wealth and abundance and the wood element. Avoid metal here, and too much lighting. Tall green candles are good. I also like to place a bowl of money in this sector, and it's also a good place for a gold money Buddha. If you have a green leafy indoor plant, this is the place to put it.

The South West sector represents romance and relationships. It is usually good to have red or pink candles here and pairs of anything, but be careful if the 5 Star or 2 Star are in the South West as you should avoid too much fire energy then.

The North West sector relates to helpful friends, general support, future wealth, and career opportunities. Electronic equipment ideally should be in the West or North West sector of your home. Healthy plants are good for this sector, as are the colors blue and black. Avoid outdoor water features here.

CLEANING

Ok, the bottom line is that Sheng Chi is good positive energy and the more happily it flows through your home, the happier and wealthier you will be. You will be prosperous, enjoy good relationships, and life will flow easily for you. Good chi does not flow where there is dust, clutter, dirt, or old cobwebs. Negative energy likes such things.

This means CLEANING! Yes, cleaning can be boring and

a drudge, but not when you realize that you are attracting prosperity and happiness to you, by simple things like cleaning away dirt, dust, cobwebs, and clearing out clutter! This also means moving furniture and cleaning under it. Once you see fast improvements in your life, you will actually look forward to cleaning! Even the least spiritually sensitive person will actually feel the difference in a house which is cleaned out!

Cleaning gets rid of negative energy and brings in positive energy.

I also like to spray essential oils in a spray bottle of water around the house. This really lifts the energy!
I also recommend cleaning with natural products such as salt and vinegar – you will be amazed how effective these are as cleaners, and without chemicals! The Chinese believe that the state of your oven is in direct relationship to the state of your finances, so give it a very good clean out, and make sure the stove top is glistening and sparking! Vinegar here is also a great help.

CINNAMON

Cinnamon is wonderful. Some Feng Shi masters advise to sprinkle cinnamon under your front door mat to attract wealth. Another wealth attractant is to tie three cinnamon sticks together with green thread and hang just inside your front door. I make a wealth and protection floor wash by boiling cinnamon and basil powder together in a saucepan, then adding that to a floor wash of nothing but salty water. Attract wealth and protect your home just by washing your floors! Now that's profitable multi-tasking!

COINS

It's a good idea to have jars of coins around the house as this symbolizes (and attracts!) abundance. You can place eight Chinese coins under your front door mat (along with sprinkled cinnamon) to attract wealth into your house. Six Chinese coins tied together with red string are good to hang in areas where the 5 and 2 Flying Stars are for the year. They are also good to counteract sickness energy so hang them in the bedroom of anyone who is sick.

COLOR

Colors are important in Feng Shi.

Red: passion. Good in the South and South East.

Pink: romance, friendship. Good in the South and South East.

Blue: healing, communication. Good in the West, North, South East, North West. Dark blue is good in the South West.

Yellow: clarity of thought.

Orange: creativity, legal matters.

Green: finances, prosperity, fertility, employment and general good luck.

Purple: spiritual insight, inspiration, power, success.

Black: to prevent harm or to get rid of something. Good in the North, South West, North West, West.

Gray: Good in the North and West.

White: cleansing, protection.

COMPASS

You need a compass to figure out where the sectors of your house are! You don't need an expensive fancy compass, just a working compass.

CRANES

Place a picture of a pair of white cranes in the South of your house to help a long happy marriage!

CRYSTALS

Crystals should be cleansed when you first purchase them to get rid of any negative energies. You can dip them in salt water then leave them out in sunlight and moonlight for at least 3 days and up to 7 days, or you can simply pass them through the smoke of a smudge stick.

CUL DE SAC

At the end of a cul de sac? Bad energy! Yes! Very bad. But you can do something about it. Houses at the end of a cul de sac have energy which is trapped, especially if there is a higher landform (human-made or natural) behind the property. This reflects in loss of income and missed opportunities. The chi rushes fast to the house at the end, and rushing chi is not good chi. What you can do is build a wall in front of your house, but a wall with a big hole in it. Even a trellis planted with some sort of flowering vine is excellent. This will help the chi slow down. Then put lots of flowering plants in front of your house, and make the pathway to your house winding.

If you can't do a wall or trellis, then place two rows of potted plants, or very healthy fruit trees, in parallel (but curving!) rows so as to create a pathway between them. If you are on a tight budget, and are doing this over an already pathed (straight) area and feel this looks strange, just get some ornamental pebbles and place along the (new) pathway. They are quite cheap. Tip – go to a big landscape place and take your own empty bags or containers to fill. This is far less expensive than buying ready-made bags of pebbles, and a fraction of the cost!

The chi will slow down, and flow happily to your home.

CUSTOMERS

Need more customers? Purchase a ringing bell with 7 metals – available online from any Feng Shui supplier if you don't have a Feng Shui shop nearby. It dramatically and quickly increases the number of customers!

D

DARK MOON

The Dark Moon is the two days before the New Moon and is the ideal time to declutter. If you are dreading attacking the clutter, just clean out one small area at this time!

DESK PLACEMENT

It is important to have a solid wall behind your desk. It's also good to have an image of a mountain behind you – just find one on the net and print it out if finances are lacking! It is also important that your desk affords you a good view of the door and the whole room. Have no clutter on your desk. Clear clutter, for a cluttered desk reflects and even causes a cluttered mind. It is ideal to have a good view out a window. An "L" shaped desk is considered fine in Feng Shui.

DIET

Avoid them, just eat less (or more healthily!) and exercise more! And walk around saying, "I can eat whatever I like and never put on excess weight!" It works! If possible, exercise first thing in the morning, as that gets it out of the way for the day. Don't think that you are losing weight, think that you are getting fitter and healthier. Start this new fitness regime with the New Moon.

DINING ROOM

Have a full fruit bowl on or near your dining table, and mirrors reflecting it are good as this is said to double your prosperity. It is also good if every family member can sit facing one of their favorable directions.

Have an even number of dining chairs, especially if you are single and looking for a relationship!

If you can, avoid a rectangular dining table and go instead for a round or square one because then every person is equidistant from each other.

The dining room is not the place to display photos or paintings of people who have passed on.

Mirrors that reflect the table and guests as well as full

bowls of fruit will bring in an abundance of wealth as well as friends.

DOORS

Doors which are hard to open, which do not open all the way, and which make a squeaky sound, are all working against your prosperity and against opportunities coming to you.

Try never to sit with your back to a door.

DRAGONS

For those people with a garden, try to have winding pathways through it, and no straight paths, as the dragon energy (highly favorable) is said to like curving pathways only. This applies to walking places in the garden whether or not they are paved. Also, the dragon energy is better if you cannot see the whole garden from any one position. If you are unable to do this, at least try to have winding pathways in the East. If you live in an apartment but have an outside area, no matter how small, place winding rows of flowering plants. Again, it is best to do this in the East.

Inside your home, it is highly favorable to place dragon images in the East sector, but make sure they are not cloisonné or other metals. Wood, ceramic, and crystal dragons are good here! You can even print out an image of a dragon and display it on the wall.

Never have a dragon image in the bedroom.

DREAMS

Keep a piece of paper and a pen by your bed, and as soon as you wake up, write down your dreams. Dreams are often forgotten within a minute or so of waking up, so it pays to write them down quickly. You will be surprised how accurate they turn out to be! Even if you can only remember things like "a red car," write that down. It may not make sense at the time, but it may make sense later.

DRIED FLOWERS

Potpourri is definitely spiritually bad! Don't even think about having it in the house! Dead and dried flowers can attract negative energy. Now, if you have a pressed flower which has special meaning to you, that is fine, as that is infused with the energy of the special meaning, but don't have bowls of potpourri or vases of dried flowers and suchlike!

E

ESSENTIAL OILS

Essential oils have been used in various spiritual disciplines over the ages.

Basil: protection, harmony, and communication.
Bergamot: prosperity, and general success.
Cinnamon: protection, to attract wealth, to attract a lover.
Ginger: courage and strength.
Lavender: healing, love.
Lemon: purification.
Mandarin: happiness.
Peppermint: luck and success.
Patchouli: excellent for attracting a lover.
Sandalwood: cleansing and protection.
Ylang Ylang: attracts romance.

EARTH

Sometimes it is good to earth ourselves. Walk outside, preferably in bare feet, and rub your feet into the ground. Walk around barefoot.

ELECTROMAGNETIC FIELDS

Don't sleep close to your cell phone or clocks. Put a piece of clear quartz on your computer or other electrical equipment and cleanse it regularly.

ELEPHANTS

Elephants symbolize wisdom and strength and it is good to have images of elephants in your home. If you have a garden statue of an elephant, try to have it facing a window. An elephant with its trunk up is said to bring good fortune and an elephant with its trunk down is said to provide protection.

ENTRANCE

This is a vital place in your house! All the energy enters here, so make your entrance as stunning and spotless as you can!

Avoid a mirror directly facing the front door as this may push the good energy straight back out. If you face a wall directly when entering your house, it is good to have a large painting of a beautiful landscape to invite opportunities into your life.

If your front door is difficult to open, squeaks, or doesn't open the whole way, fix this immediately, as this can block prosperity and opportunities.

It is not good to have something such as a tree in alignment with the front door. To remedy this, some say to place a Bagua mirror over the door.

The path to the front door should be even – as in not narrow here, much wider there – and curving. Avoid straight lines leading to your front door. Curved lines encourage good chi, straight lines do not. If you do have a straight path to your front door, you can remedy this by placing pots of flowers along the path at intervals. If you have to walk in a winding way to get to your front door, the chi will move that way too, and this is good. If where you live is too cold, you can use ornamental rocks, or anything else you can think of! Be inventive! Just be aware that straight paths are not auspicious.

It is a good idea to have the entrance to your house very well lit. You can use garden lights.

EVIL EYE

The Evil Eye figures in many ancient cultures, and blue beads are used against it. The Bedouins used to tie blue beads to the halters of their Arabian horses to ward off the Evil Eye. The Greeks for centuries gave babies a blue bracelet to ward off the Evil Eye.

The Evil Eye basically means someone has focused too intently on you – usually with jealousy – but the point is too much focus. It is usually always unintentional. It can be fixed with Evil Eye bracelets or other jewelry, and these are readily available everywhere. Even having an image of a painted blue eye shape works.

F

FENCES

It is important to have a fence behind your house. If you live in an apartment, put a painting of a mountain on your back wall. I speak about this under the heading "Black Turtle." If you find money comes in, but you cannot hang onto it for some reason, go build a wall or fence and you will be amazed at the difference! This happened to me. I moved into a house with no back fence, and the neighbors behind me had a spare open block. Well, there was a wire fence, but it was flimsy. Money came in but went right back out for all sorts of bizarre reasons. I bought some cheap bamboo screening and put it behind the house, and the effect on my finances was astounding!

FISH

Fish are great to activate good chi. You do have to be careful where you place them! If you don't have a Feng Shui consultant, never mind, just play this by ear. If your finances are not going well and you have followed everything else in this book, move your aquarium. If finances pick up quickly, leave it there! Try different positions until you find the right one, the right one meaning your finances are going well. Many Feng Shui consultants believe the ideal number of goldfish is eight gold and one black. The gold fish are for prosperity and the black one is for protection. If you already have goldfish of any number or color, don't stress!

FIVE ELEMENT PAGODA

If you are into Feng Shui items, this is good to place where the Flying Star 5 is for the particular year. It is called a Five Element Pagoda because the 5 different shapes, one on top of the other, represent the five elements. The square at the bottom represents earth, which in turn produces metal which in turn produces water, which in turn produces wood which in turn produces fire. The top usually unscrews so you can put dirt from your garden in it. If you live in an apartment and have no dirt, that's fine!

FLOWERS

Make sure that any flowers in the house are not dying as

this will attract bad chi called "Killing Chi" (yuk!!) and that you replace the water every day. Smelly old water and dying flowers do not attract good energy!

Lots of flowers outside the house mean wealth! Flowers bring auspicious energy.

FLOWER REMEDIES

Most people have heard of Bach Flower Remedies – particularly Rescue Remedy – and Australian Flower Essences among others. There is a remedy for most things.

Dr Bach, a medical doctor and bacteriologist, developed his remedies in the first half of the 20th century to treat 38 negative states of mind. The Australian Bush Flower Essences were developed by 5th generation herbalist Ian White, who developed 64 essences targeting issues related to modern-day living, such as jet-lag, exam nerves or psychic attack.

Flower Remedies are good to have on hand!

FLUTES

When hanging bamboo flutes, make sure that the

mouthpiece is up. People hang them from exposed beams at a right angle, so that they form a triangle to the beam. They are said to be a remedy for exposed beams. Bamboo flutes are also said to be good for the stability of your wealth and for the security of your home, so are good to place near the front door and near anything that means money.

FRIDGE

Your fridge reflects prosperity, so needs to be full as well as spotless. Clutter in the fridge is bad for your finances, and as for stale food! Horrors! Imagine what that is doing to your prosperity! Any bad odors in the house are very, very bad for chi, so get rid of them! Clean out your fridge on a regular basis. It is nice to wipe out your fridge with essential oil of vanilla, if you can find it. It can be hard to get. If you can't get vanilla essential oil, don't use a chemical substitute, wipe out your fridge with lavender essential oil instead.

Make sure the outside of the fridge is clean and not covered in dirty hand marks, even if you have to follow the kids every time they open the door and wipe it over! You will be pleased at the state of your finances if you do!

FRONT DOOR

The front door is of vital importance in both Feng Shui and Vastu Shastra as the house gets its chi nourishment through the front door. The front door should have no peeling paint, and should be very clean and nicely painted. It should not squeak when opened, and must be well cared for. There should be no obstructions in front of the door. The entrance to your house should be as beautiful as possible. The better your house or apartment entrance, the better success, good luck, and health you will enjoy.

If you have another door to your house, use the front door instead as this is more auspicious. Curving paths are good, straight paths are not good. If there is a straight path to your door, place potted flowering plants along it here and there to make the energy curve along the path.

If the main door has other doors along the same wall, keep the other doors closed at all times.

FRUIT

If you have a bowl of fruit in the house, you must see that it is full at all times as a partially empty fruit bowl will lead to a lack of abundance! This represents wealth, so keep it full!

FRUIT TREES

Any fruit bearing tree is considered a symbol of abundance.

G

GARAGE

I suppose by now you realize what I am going to say. Your garage cannot be cluttered! Yes I know it is hard when you need somewhere to store stuff, but there is a difference between clean, organized storage, and clutter! All storage in the garage needs to be, and look, organized, and leave room around it to sweep and clean. Make sure there are no old cobwebs. Spray it frequently with the air spray mentioned in this book, and also smudge it more regularly than you smudge your house.

GARBAGE

If you have garbage stored somewhere, take a look at what sector of the house this represents (such as South East = wealth, South West – relationships, and so on) as this is where you have blockages in your life! Get rid of garbage, don't have it hanging around!!

GEOMANCY

Geomancy means the figuring out of the energies of nature. Geopathic stress means "earth suffering" and refers to places of negative energies usually associated with electromagnetic fields. Most people know about negative energies due to electromagnetic fields near high voltage wires. Interestingly, ants, termites, and wasps like to make their nests along lines of geopathic stress, and cats even like to lie on them!

CITRUS ESSENTIAL OILS

Lemon, grapefruit, or orange essential oils are great to

make into spray and spray around the room when you need motivation. They also clear the mind.

H

HERBS

Angelica - protects children.

Anise – increases psychic abilities, wards off the Evil Eye.

Basil - protection and clearing negative energies, attracts wealth and success, and a happy home. Wards off the Evil Eye. A good protection plant to grow around the house.

Bay Leaves - for protection, and keeps away evil and jinxes.

Bergamot - attracts success and prosperity.

Betony - reverses hexes, and provides protection from disease and evil entities.

Black Cohosh (also called Black Snake Root) - very strong general protection and strengthens those who are shy or weak.

Black Pepper – said to provide protection against witches. Also said to get rid of evil and to remove someone who is being an obstacle to you.

Blessed Thistle - protects the home from evil.

Boneset (also called White Snake Root) - reverses jinxes and protects against unnatural illnesses.

Boldo - keeps away bad customers and disruptive people, repels evil spirits and diseases.

Borage – peace in the home.

Burdock Root - protection, cleansing from evil, reverses curses.

Caraway seed - protection for young children.

Chamomile – good for a floor wash as a spiritual cleanser. Removes jinxes.

Cinnamon – attracts love, luck, and money. Also protection.

Clover Flowers, Red – ensures marital fidelity, and a prosperous marriage.

Clover Flowers, White – drives away evil. Personal protection.

Comfrey Root - for protection when traveling.

Comfrey Leaf – helps you hold onto the money that you have. If you don't have a back fence, comfrey is ideal to grow in a row behind your house.

Coriander Seeds – draws new love to you, and keeps your lover faithful to you.

Cubeb Berries – will draw new love to you.

Cumin Seeds - keeps your lover faithful to you, keeps evil and bad luck away from your house.

Damiana – powerful attractant for new lover.

Devil's Shoestrings - will help get a job, reverses evil spells, protects from gossip.

Dill Leaf – helps those jinxed in love.

Dragon's Blood – attracts wealth.

Elder Flowers – sprinkle around house, or carry – protects from criminals and from the law.

Eucalyptus – protection, and clearing negative energies.

Fennel Seeds –protection from the law. General protection. Increases a woman's courage.

Fenugreek Seed - carry with your money to attract wealth. Also helps monetary windfalls and luck with money.

Five Finger Grass - wards off evil, and provides safety for traveling.

Flax Seed – increases psychic ability, protection of children.

Garlic – powerfully protective against all kinds of evil.

Gentian Root – a powerful herb to attract a lover.

Ginger Root – protects against evil magic and hots up your live life!

Golden Seal – brings wisdom and strength and promotes better health.

Horehound - protection from wild dogs.

Hyssop - spiritual cleanser. Hyssop was used to sprinkle water or blood in purification rites by the ancient Israelites.

Jasmine Flowers – helps psychic dreams.

Lavender - protects home, marriage, promotes friendship, love, romance and harmony. Can be used as a smudge. A good protection plant to grow around the house.

Lemon Grass - highly protective.

Lovage Root - to attract a lover, only a lover of the opposite gender.

Magnolia Leaves – placed under the mattress for marital fidelity and happiness and mutual sexual attraction.

Marjoram – protects home and business from jinxes.

Mint – attracts money. Breaks hoodoo spells and jinxes.

Motherwort - protection of mothers and children.

Mugwort –protection, very strong for cleansing negative energies and getting rid of curses.

Nettle – a strong jinx breaker if dried and then sprinkled.

Nutmeg – helps win money by gambling.

Oregano – keeps the law away.

Patchouli – excellent to attract a lover. The leaf draws a lover as well as money, and breaks jinxes.

Pennyroyal – keeps and restores peace in the home.

Peppermint - protects from enemies, reverses curses, and attracts wealth, attracts luck and success.

Pine – cleansing, removes negative energies, draws steady money.

Raspberry Leaves – used by women in a bath to ensure fidelity from their men.

Rose - excellent for romance, and to attract a lover.

Rose Petals – will reverse any love spell someone has cast against you.

Rosemary – protects the home.

Rue - reverses curses, and is cleansing. Rue is good to use in a bath to break spells.

Safflower leaves – good for gay men to burn for love.

Sage - a white sage smudge stick cleanses the home of negativity and bad energies and entities.

Sandalwood – a strong protection and also clears negative energies.

Slippery Elm Bark – stops malicious gossip against you.

Snake Weed – protects against false friends.

Star Anise – protection, prevents bad luck, brings back a lost lover.

Sulfur – protection.

Tansy – prevents tax office or police looking into one's affairs!!

Thyme – increases wealth and makes it stay with you.

Vervain/ Verbena – protection, and draws a lover to you.

Wintergreen – attracts good luck and money.

Wormwood - safe travel, and personal safety. Increase psychic ability.

Yarrow – breaks curses and increases psychic power.

Ylang Ylang - attracts and keeps a lover.

HELPFUL PEOPLE AND SUPPORT

The North West sector of your house is to do with support from people, as well as career opportunities. This is a good place to have green leafy plants, especially those with blue flowers. You can also hang images which mean support and help, such as images of angels.

HOME OFFICE

If you have a home office, sit with a solid wall behind your back. While sitting at your desk, it is also good to have a full view of the room with the door in front of you. Your desk should be free from clutter. It's fine to have your desk piled high while you are working on something, but organize this as soon as you finish.

Try to have your desk facing one of your favorable directions.

HORSES

Horses have strong (and good!) chi, and it's good to have images of horses either singularly, or in a group of eight. They are good as symbols for business, and represent success, power and speed. If you have a single horse, have a fast galloping horse, or a horse carrying treasures. Do not have an image of a rearing horse.

J

JASMINE

Jasmine smells beautiful. If you are growing it in your garden, just make sure it doesn't choke any other plants!

K

KITCHEN

If your stove and fridge are next to each other, try to have some wood in between them, otherwise the fire element and water elements will clash. If your stove and kitchen sink are opposite each other, put a green rug on the floor. As I say elsewhere in this book, the stove is directly related to your finances so make sure all the elements work and you use them in turn. One of the worst things you can do for your finances is to have a dirty stove or a non-working burner. Some people recommend having a mirror to reflect the hot plates on the stove, in the belief that this will increase prosperity. However, traditional Feng Shui believes it is bad to have the cooking reflected, as it will cause accidents.

KNIVES

Keep knives and sharp pointy objects in drawers, and never display them on a bench top. They have cutting energy and this is not auspicious. It's best not to display knifes and scissors in the kitchen. Never give knives or pointed sharp objects (even knitting needles) as gifts. If someone gives you a knife as a gift, give them a couple of coins back – this is supposed to take away the bad energy!

L

LAVENDER

Lavender essential oil is wonderful to put in your final rinse for your laundry, and is also wonderful to put in your bath. You can also add a few drops to a bottle of olive oil or almond oil (or any oil you choose!) to make a lovely body oil. Lavender incense smells heavenly too!

Lavender oil was used in ancient Egyptian ritual cleansing magic. In ancient Roman times, lavender flowers sold for hugely high prices. The ancient Roman natural historian, Pliny, said that it was formerly believed that asps made their homes in lavender, so the plants should be approached with great caution.

Lavender flowers can be put between the pillow and the pillow case to bring happy dreams and a good night's sleep. You can also use dried lavender to smudge your house. Lavender has many uses – protection, cleansing, anti-stress, an attractant for a lover.

LEAKY TAPS

Gradual loss of income, and who wants that!

LEMON GRASS

Lemon grass has been used as a smudge. It is said to ward

off evil and bring good luck in love. It is good to use in floor wash for protection, and also if you want to sell or rent your house or apartment.

LIONS

Lions are good for a business if placed in front of the door, but not inside a building and certainly not inside a home. If you are born in the year of the pig, rooster, rabbit or goat, avoid lions! Lions are said to ward off thieves and loss of income from the business.

LIVING ROOM

Just make sure your furniture is not blocking the flow of energy in your living room. If you can move around it freely, and preferably in curved lines, then the auspicious chi will too. Have beautiful items you love in your living room.

LOOKING FOR LOVE?

Is the South West sector of your home missing? If so, place a statue, a large rock, or large ceramic pot at the point where the corner of the room would have been if it were not missing!

LOPAN

A Lopan is beautiful Chinese compass used in Feng Shui.

M

MANDARIN DUCKS

If you are into Feng Shui items and are in a relationship, then go buy a pair of Mandarin Ducks! I don't mean real ones, of course! Mandarin Ducks mate for life and so are regarded as a symbol of married-forever-bliss in married couples. Always have them in pairs. If you are looking for love, they are also good. Place them in the bedroom on the bedside table. Even images of them on the walls are good – just google an image of them and print it out.

MERCURY RETROGRADE

Do not buy a house, or sign any contracts when Mercury

is retrograde, no matter how much of a good idea it seems at the time!

MIRRORS

Mirrors must not be placed in the bedroom, or in the entrance directly in front of the front door, or reflecting any plumbing in the bathroom.

MONEY TOAD

The three legged money toad is said to be auspicious. Don't place it directly in front of the front door. Feng Shui masters are divided as to whether it can face the front door or not, so try it and see if it works for you. Feng Shui results are usually fast, so it won't take you long to figure out!

MUGWORT

Mugwort is Artemisia Vulgaris so don't confuse it with Wormwood which is Artemisia Absinthe. I am a BIG fan of smudging my house with mugwort– it is said to be far stronger than white sage as a smudge stick to clear away any negative energies directed at you by a person.

It also doesn't smell as strong as white sage – not that I mind the smell of white sage smudge sticks at all!

If you want psychic dreams, put fresh or dried mugwort in between the pillow case and the pillow as this will induce psychic dreams – however, if you are an empath you will have more empathic dreams, and so on! Not so great if an ex boyfriend who treated you badly but wants you back is missing you dreadfully! If anyone has it in for you, you will also be aware of this. These experiences may not be pleasant in the middle of the night! Bear in mind it may take a week or at least a few nights of sleeping with mugwort in your pillow case for this to happen.

Mugwort is used in moxibustion in acupuncture to raise levels of chi, to strengthen the blood, and to maintain general health. Its best known use is to reverse the position of breech babies (this is generally by using a moxa stick to smudge parts of the woman's feet by the acupuncturist) and scientific studies have shown it is effective in this.

N

NEW CAREER OR PROJECT

If you are having trouble with a new career or a new project, head straight for the West sector of your house and give it a very good clean!

NO AND NOT

When saying affirmations or even speaking normal words in everyday life, it is important to notice your use of the words "no," "not," and all such words.

As I said in my books on affirmations, affirmations and even ordinary words we speak should contain no negative words such as "no" or "not," and affirmations must always be stated in the present or past tense.

Here are some examples.
Wrong.
My car does not break down.
Right.
My car always runs well.

Wrong.

I will soon have enough money.

Right.

I have enough money now.

It's not just affirmations, it is general speech, your everyday words. Get used to saying positive things, both in and out of your house! For this reason I do not like to watch the news, as it is full of bad energy, bad news, and awful things. Just be aware of EVERYTHING that is said in your house, whether it comes from the television, radio, you, your family, or guests!

Remember that it does not matter what you MEAN, it ONLY matters what you SAY.

Try to state everything in the positive. You should not say, "I am never going to argue with my neighbors."
What will this statement attract?
An argument with your neighbors!

Yes, the statement does *mean* the right thing but it must be *said* in the positive sense.

There are universal laws that are very rigid and go by what you SAY not what you MEAN!

O

ORANGE TREES

Orange trees represent prosperity, happiness, and good luck.

P

PEACH BLOSSOM LOVE

This is a famous, or infamous, Feng Shi remedy to attract partners to your life! It will attract quantity not quality, so use some discernment when all the suitors start piling in!

You need to know your Day Pillar using the Four Pillars technique.

Now, do NOT use this if you are already in a relationship – I suppose that's an obvious thing to say – but don't make the mistake of thinking it will improve your current relationship. It won't, it will just draw in new ones!
You need to find your Day Pillar by going to the following website and entering your hour and date of birth. If you don't know the hour, that doesn't matter, as it is the Day animal you need to find.

http://www.angelandpsychicbooks.com/Feng_Shui.php

Have your Day Pillar? (Animal?) Good. Now you will need a jar of water. Some Feng Shi consultants say you need a vase of flowers or an image of flowers and so on, but I recently attended a seminar in Malaysia with one of the world's current leading Feng Shui masters, and he said that this is a misunderstanding of the water element. He said all you need is water. So when you know your Day Pillar animal, look at the table below, and place your jar of water within the 30 degrees on the compass direction. Obviously, you need a compass for this, and also stand in the center of your house to get the direction.

Peach Blossom Romance Location Finder

255° - 285° Rat, Dragon, or Monkey.

165° - 195° Ox, Snake, or Rooster.

75° - 105° Tiger, Horse, or Dog.

345° - 15° Rabbit, Sheep, or Pig.

Again, do NOT confuse this with your year of birth! If you are, for example, a Chinese Astrology Tiger, that has nothing to do with your Peach Blossom Direction. You need to look up the animal of your DAY PILLAR.

PERIOD EIGHT.

In February 2004, there was a change in 20 year periods. We are now in Period Eight. Take advantage of this good 8 energy by having items grouped together in numbers of eight, even by displaying the number 8 in your walls in the form of artwork!

PETS

Pets are wonderful, but pet smells are not!

PHOENIX

Is the bringer of opportunities and is particularly

beneficial to bring luck when the situation appears hopeless. It may also represent peace and prosperity. Hang a picture of the phoenix and the dragon for martial happiness.

PHOTOS

Don't have photos of your ex hanging around! If you split up with him and he hurt you, he isn't The One, and you need to move on!

Don't have photos of people who have passed on in your dining room. Don't put photos of people above fireplaces or heaters unless the fireplaces or heaters are not used.

Photos of happy couples are good for the South West sector of the house. Only have happy photos in your house, photos that represent happiness, love, and wealth. Avoid unhappy photos at all costs!

PLANTS

Avoid cacti, as these are said not to be auspicious, as are plants with spiky leaves. Weeping plants and trees such as weeping willows are said to attract sadness to a house. In the South East corner of your home, have plants with round leaves to represent coins.

At all costs, avoid creeping plants such as ivy over your front gate or front door. This is extremely bad and signifies severe loss of income, and even loss of the house.

POISON ARROWS

This is the name for straight lines that produce bad energy when directed at your house. If you have a tree in direct alignment with your front door, this tree is said to be a poison arrow as it will cause Sha Chi (negative energy) to be directed at your house.

Q

QI

Another way to write "chi" or "ki," energy life force of all living things and even objects. Think of Tai Chi or Aikido.

Feng Shui works on energy in the home and Acupuncture works on energy in the body.

QUICK LOVE FIX

Declutter the South West sector of your house! Place red candles there. Make your bedroom beautiful.

QUICK PROSPERITY FIX

Declutter the South West sector of your house and then clean your stove!

R

RED BIRD

The Red Bird represents the front of your home and the opportunities that come into your life. It is important to make this as beautiful as possible, and this will bring beautiful chi and hence wonderful opportunities into your life.

ROCKS

For abundance and stability, place a pile of rocks at the 4 corners of your house.

ROOSTERS

If you are born in the year of the rabbit, avoid images of roosters in your house.

ROSE OIL

If you have suffered a breakup, burn rose incense, put rose essential oil in an oil burner, take a bath in which you have put essential rose oil, and you will feel so much better! Try it, it really works!

Rose essential oil also attracts a new lover fast.

ROSES

It is not good to give someone roses, especially red roses, if they have thorns as this will cause prickles in your relationship! Luckily, thornless roses are available these days!

The South area of your garden is the ideal place for a rose garden.

S

SHEETS

It is best to have natural unbleached fibers for your sheets, and wash them in organic cleaners. Avoid chemicals wherever you can! If you can, dry them in the sun as this is great chi and is also cleansing. However, don't ever leave anything out overnight as this absorbs negative energy.

I like to add lavender essential oil to the finishing rinse of my sheets.

SHOES

I have seen some people who have an otherwise beautiful house but leave a disgusting pile of shoes directly inside the front door. This is awful, as the entrance is where the chi comes in, and good chi won't stay around with a pile of shoes right there! Remove them! Have a rack somewhere for them.

SHOWER

Get a shower filter which removes chlorine and all other nasties from the water, and you will smell beautiful and feel really good! Remember to change the filter about once a year.

SMUDGING

Mugwort is a most powerful smudge stick, but white sage is powerful as well. You can even smudge with lavender if you want. Smudge sticks are cheap, but oh so effective!! After you have decluttered and scrubbed, you get to smudge. It feels wonderful! Remember to smudge corners and behind doors, and to smudge drawers and cupboards. If you have had an area which was cluttered, give that a really good smudge. I like to ring bells before I smudge – you can find these at any Feng Shui shop, either a bricks and mortar shop or online, they are readily available.

SALT

Use sea salt every time. It is highly spiritually cleansing – sprinkle it all over the floor before you vacuum, put salt in every corner of your house, bathe in sea salt (well, sea salt added to your bath water that is!), even put a line of salt across your doors and windows for protection!

A widely used cure for the Flying Star 5 and 2 energies is to put 1/3 glass of sea salt into glass, then fill it with water. Some people add 6 Chinese coins. Place in the corner in the areas which have the 5 Star and 2 Star energies for the year. It will absorb all negativity. Be careful not to disturb it, and simply vacuum around it. You will need to top up the water at regular intervals. If you have cats, you will find they love to drink the salty water! Strange, but don't forget that cats love to lie on areas of geopathic stress.

SHA CHI

This is negative energy, you don't want it! You will find it where you find clutter, cobwebs, dirt, dust, garbage, bad smells, and straight lines.

SHENG CHI

This is GOOD energy! You will find it where you have lovely smells, no clutter, cleanliness, happy images, lovely music, curved lines.

SKYLIGHTS

Excellent everywhere but the bedroom.

SINGING BOWL

Wonderful to ring a few times a day in the sectors where the flying Stars 5 and 2 are for the year.

SPACE CLEARING

The actual term "space clearing" is recent in the scheme of things, but the concept is ancient. Several cultures advocate the space clearing of your house. The method I mention here is most effective!

First clean your house, even if it takes a couple of days! Remove all clutter. If you don't have time to get to ALL of it, store some of it in boxes and stack these neatly. Next, sprinkle salt over your carpet then vacuum it, and then sprinkle sandalwood essential oils around it. Sprinkle salt all over your floors then sweep or vacuum them.

The next step is to boil some cinnamon in a saucepan. Put this in a bucket of very hot water with sea salt added to it, and sandalwood essential oils. Wash your floors with this. The next step is to clap your hands and/or ring metal bells or a Chinese singing bowl all around the house, particularly in corners. Make sure you do this over any storage and in cupboards and drawers as well.

The next step is to get a sage smudge stick. Light it, then walk all though your house waving it around. It is very important to pay particular attention to the corners, starting low in the corner and smudging all the way up to the ceiling. Negative energy likes to collect in corners. If you have a room which had been cluttered before you did an awesome job decluttering it, spend more time smudging this! While you are smudging, leave the windows in each room open at least a little bit to let the negative energy out. Be sure to smudge every drawer and every cupboard, EVERYWHERE!!

After you have smudged the whole house (and smudging should be done weekly, by the way), get some sea salt and place a little bit in the corner of each room. You don't need to put enough to be seen, a sprinkle will do. If there is furniture pushed up against a corner, you can throw more sea salt behind it.

There. You're done! Doesn't the place feel great! The difference will be noticeable!

Now you can go even further and use your essential oils and water spray bottle – see below - to spray through the house. You can also burn incense – cleansing incense includes frankincense, pine, Nag Champa, and sandalwood.

SPRAY

Make your own spray mists for the house by buying a simple cheap spray bottle, filling it with water and adding a few drops of essential oil, then giving it a good shake! Use basil, eucalyptus, or sandalwood for protection and clearing negative energies, lemongrass to attract good luck and remove negative energies, peppermint to protect from enemies as well as attracting luck and success, bergamot for success and prosperity, mint for money, Ylang Ylang or rose for romance, patchouli to attract romance, and lavender for general healing and happiness.

STAIRCASE

Feng Shui says that you should not have your staircase directly facing your front door or your prosperity and the good energy will come in and then go straight out (or up!) If it does, place a potted plant in the way.

STOVE

As I said, the stove and oven must be spotlessly clean as this is directly related to finances. It is also a good idea to use the burners on the stove in turn so that they receive equal use.

TOYS

Toys to do with war and war themes are bad energy, so if your child has any, put them away after use.

TROUBLE CONCEIVING

If you are having trouble conceiving, position your

bedhead against the wall which is the man's favorable Romance direction. Earlier in the book I set out your Kua calculator. These are the favorable Romance directions for a man according to his Kua number.

1 - South

2 – North West

3 – South East

4 - East

5 – North West

6 – South West

7 – North East

8 - West

9 – North

U

UNFAITHFULNESS

Avoid unfaithfulness in your relationship by getting rid of any mirrors that face the bed. Also, check that you don't have any water placed in your partner's Peach Blossom

Direction! (See "Peach Blossom" in this book.)

A dip in the ground outside your house to the West can cause unfaithfulness. This also applies if you have a basement situated in the West. In either case, hang a brass bell there and ring it as often as you can!

Also, it is super important to make sure there is no clutter in the North East sector of your house as well as your bedroom.

V

VANILLA

Men are said to love the scent of Vanilla! The Body Shop makes a lovely Vanilla scent! If you can get the essential oils of vanilla, wipe your fridge with it but don't use a chemical substitute.

Mix alfalfa and cinnamon with vanilla, add a little bit of magnetic sand, and this is said to attract material possessions. Vanilla oil mixed with strawberry oil and orange oil is said to reverse bad luck if sprinkled around the house.

W

WATER BEDS

These are not a good idea due to their electromagnetic field. They are yang, and thus not good for the bedroom.

WATER FEATURES

Moving water activates the chi in the area. This is usually either very good or very bad - no middle road! If you have a water feature and your finances are good, leave it there, but if not, experiment with different positions and see when your finances pick up.

Water features should always flow towards the house.

WATER PIPES

If water pipes leak, this symbolizes your money leaking away from you.

In the bathroom, place a rock near any water pipes to prevent loss of income, and tie a red string around the pipes.

WINDCHIMES

Wind chimes generate good chi. Metal wind chimes are not so good in the South East. A wind chime with 6 rods is great to counteract the Flying Star 5 energy.

WINDOWS

Windows need to be clean as clean windows attract opportunities into your life. A large tree or bush directly outside a window is said to be inauspicious.

Windows should open outwards rather than opening inwards or sliding up and down or sideways. Not much you can do about that, unless you are building a house! Just keep them sparkling and spotless, and remove any shrubbery pressing on a window.

WU-LU

The Wu-Lu (as mentioned above under "Calabash" which is another name for it) is a gourd and needs to have a hole in the top to absorb sickness energy. It is good to place where the Flying Star 2 is for the year, or in the bedroom of anyone not feeling well. It is preferable to use an actual gourd rather than a brass imitation of a gourd.

YLANG YLANG

Ylang Ylang essential oil is wonderfully sensual. Men love it! Ylang Ylang is also wonderful for cleansing and protecting the house – use it in a floor wash, in a spray bottle mixed with water, in your bath as an aura cleanser (best to add sea salt and Epsom Salts as well) – anywhere you can use an essential oil, you can use Ylang Ylang! Put some drops into Almond Oil for a wonderful body oil!

3. You're on your way to health, wealth and love!

The ancient Chinese said there are 3 types of luck:
1) Heaven Luck
2) Earth Luck
3) Human Luck.

With Heaven Luck, you're stuck with it! It's your destiny, there's nothing you can do about it.

Human Luck means the hard work and effort you put into your achievements and the decisions you make. You are of course fully in control of this.

Earth Luck is how the environment impacts upon you. With this book, you can do quick and easy things to help your Earth Luck! Sometimes things go wrong just because of Earth Luck, and if this is the case, then fixing the energy in the house will bring change, sometimes so fast you will be amazed!